ADVANCE PRAISE FOR *NEW RIVER BREAKDOWN*

"Not only is Terry Kennedy's *New River Breakdown* a stellar volume of prose poems, but it's also a canny primer on that genre—a many-headed, oft-misunderstood hybrid. His querulous, introspective speaker resists his own breakdown by breaking down his universe into parcels of incremental wonder in which 'fear and love [are] one and the same.' The result is poem after poem of fabulous imagery and infinite possibility. We recognize in these tableaux the worlds we inhabit and long for at once—articulated so memorably in 'What Love Comes To': 'One small thing I still love about you is how little of you I actually know . . .' Kennedy expertly explores the prose poem's accommodating elasticity, beautifully marrying the discursive brunt of the best prose and the impressionistic language verse thrives on."

Joseph Bathanti, Poet Laureate of North Carolina

"Beautiful and moving, Terry Kennedy's second poetry collection describes an elusive and haunting narrative of loss, love, and recovery. His prose poems bring us so close to the narrator that we share in our bones his predicament of wanting to go forward while fearing what may be ahead. 'It's neither the end nor the beginning of all we hope for,' he discovers. Lyricism and considered thought are here, and lines that strike sparks from these passionate poems."

Kelly Cherry, author of The Life and Death of Poetry: Poems

"Terry Kennedy's poems are taut, rich, and deeply American. If poems were on the radio like songs, it would be [his] poems you'd listen to on an all-night drive across the country to find the one you can no longer live without."

Thomas Lux, winner of the Kingsley Tufts Award for Poetry, author of Child Made of Sand

"The bright, swiftly kinetic surfaces of Terry Kennedy's poems whisper as they pass a wistful but passionate love story. He has an Impressionist's purpose and deftness of touch. I think of Renoir, of the etudes of Debussy. Yet his strophes stand firmly on their ground and are as strong as the seasons they portray. His every image bears the nuances of a remembrance. *New River Breakdown* is a rare treasure."

Fred Chappell, winner of the Bollingen Prize for Poetry, author of Ancestors and Others

"Prepare to be haunted by the poems within Terry Kennedy's *New River Breakdown*, their shifting imagery, tones, and shadings. Prepare to be mystified by how these poems flow so effortlessly beyond the description of 'prose poem' into a genre that defies any label whatsover, poems that eddy into dreamtime. 'In the dream, there is a forgotten pasture I can't stop finding' Kennedy writes, wonderingly, near the end. For us too, 'this steady pulse to look beyond the world [we] knew,' never ceases to whisper to us that the world we think we know pulses like a quasar and beckons us onward toward 'revelation,' if we can call it that. Terry Kennedy would likely call it, simply, poetry. Poetry that calls anyone who reads it to cast off the scales that cover our senses and walk into a shimmering, longed-for world."

Kathryn Stripling Byer, Poet Laureate Emerita, author of Descent and Wildwood Flower

"Terry Kennedy's brilliant conceits bring to mind John Donne in this achingly beautiful lament of a lost love. *New River Breakdown* is—in the fullness of the word—sublime."

Ron Rash, author of Waking

New River Breakdown

New River Breakdown

Terry Kennedy

Unicorn Press / Greensboro 2013

Copyright © 2013 by Terry L. Kennedy

Second printing

Library of Congress Cataloging-in-Publication Data

Kennedy, Terry L.
    New river breakdown / Terry Kennedy.
    pages cm
    ISBN 978-0-87775-900-3 (pbk. : acid-free paper)
    ISBN 978-0-87775-901-0 (cloth : acid-free paper)

    I. Title.

PS3611.E63N49 2013   811'.6—DC23   2013-017963

∞

This book is printed on Mohawk Superfine, which is
acid-free and meets ANSI standards for archival permanence.

Printed in the United States of America

Unicorn Press
1212 Grove Street
Greensboro, NC 27403

www.unicorn-press.org

for Cynthia

Half of the time we're gone but we don't know where.
PAUL SIMON

Acknowledgments

Many thanks to the editors of the following journals in which many of these poems, sometimes in different versions or with different titles, first appeared:

Border Crossing, Cave Wall, "Hoppenthaler's Congeries" at *Connotation Press: An Online Artifact, from the Fishouse, Heavy Feather Review, O. Henry Magazine, Prime Number Magazine, Roger, storySouth, THRUSH Poetry Journal, Ucity Review*, and *Waccamaw*.

Also, several of these poems first appeared in the limited edition chapbook Until the Clouds Shatter the Light That Plates our Lives, published by Jeanne Duval Editions and Poetry@ TECH. Thanks to Thomas Lux and Travis Denton for that wonderful program.

I also wish to thank the Virginia Center for the Creative Arts for fellowships that supported the conception, drafting, and revision of many of these poems.

I would be remiss if I didn't thank Andrew Saulters and Tristan Miller for the beautiful design and careful construction of the book. You have my greatest admiration.

I owe great debts to my friends and teachers for their insights, guidance, and encouragement: Dan Albergotti, Fred Chappell, Stuart Dischell, A. Van Jordan, Michael Parker, Drew Perry, Jeff Towne, Natasha Trethewey, and Lee Zacharias. And in memoriam, Jake Adam York.

To Jim Clark and Julie Funderburk, who had faith in me back when this all started, my endless thanks.

And finally, to Cynthia, my wife and best friend, whose encouragement, support, and inspiration made this book possible, I offer my deepest gratitude and love beyond words.

New River Breakdown

*

Morning, Minnesott   5
You Are Not a Stranger Here   6
The Known World   7
Pursuit of a Wound   8
Love in Another Season   9
Shadow of Sirius   10
What Love Comes To   14
American Woman   15
Tree of Smoke   16
Summer Sutra   19
Unlocking the Air   20
Breaking the Glass   21
Sometimes Winter Comes
    When You Least Expect It   22
Explorers   23
Train Dreams   28
New River Breakdown   29
Music Like Dirt   30

* *

Man on the Moon   33
The Echo Maker   34
Maps & Atlases   35
Daydream Believer   36
Like Rain on a Sunny Day   37
Tin   38
Midnight Salvage   39
Watching the Spring Festival   40
Listen   41

* * *

The Common Man   45
The Bright Forever   46
Delight & Shadows   47
In Other Rooms, Other Wonders   48
Sand & Gravel   49
The Surrendered   50
Practical Gods   51
Silence   52
Where I'm Calling From   53
How Long?   54
Harbor   58
Complicated Mathematics   59
Time & Material   60
Different Hours   61
Evidence of Things Unseen   62
Waiting   63
Servant of the Map   64

New River Breakdown

I've had some time to think about you
And watch the sun sink like a stone
PATTI GRIFFIN

Morning, Minnesott

It is morning and the pelicans are filling the sky; they glide silently past—stare at the choppy river below. The right cuff of my pants is soaked as we walk up the beach together. I say *together* but she is far ahead of me—slender and fleet—a spring doe skimming the sand. The game we play is an ancient one—you know the name, you made the rules. A crab at the edge of the pier clacks his blue claws and scowls. And the gulls diving from the sky are maniacal—compelled by greed, they fall—gleaming white missiles. She is so far ahead of me now that I plan for tomorrow. The pelicans—ugly with patience and wisdom—glide gently past. The hungover fishermen finish their coffee; pull on their rubber boots. Around the bend, the ferry churns the dark water white—gives three long bellows of its horn.

You Are Not a Stranger Here

I can imagine how one could feel trapped here—scrape &
squeal of the train as it slows but never stops or the doleful
whimper of a dog chained to the yard—its heavy padlock
keeping love & loneliness both at an admirable distance; but
it's hard to understand why you see this everywhere: in the
honk & wave of a neighbor driving up the street or the fresh-
waxed shimmer of another's car. The morning sun filters the
hedges and I cannot help but wonder why we feel compelled
to share with anyone; so please forgive me if I go back to late
last spring, how the breeze paused, then pushed the camellia
bloom in my direction, giving nod, like the slow-steady creak
of the porch swing, to some new passage.

The Known World

How often I feel all I could say has been written already or
you've heard it from folks with enlivening accents or whiter
teeth than mine—so why should I say anything at all?
Sometimes though, I try to remind myself how that small
white boat alone on the smooth blue bay is somehow more
meaningful than the untamed meadow of umbrellas & bikinis
kissing the edge of the water; or else, I think to remember
how the chef, his kitchen twitching with fish, freshly ground
cardamom, cumin, and coriander, still reaches for a finger of
salt before releasing his steaming tureens to the table; and that
should be enough—except that I know someone else who's
craved your scent, your voice, your mouth before me—and
done so beautifully.

Pursuit of a Wound

You don't slip in so much as you are pulled, deep into summer, deep into the green of the fields, every yellow tassel whispering a promise, hurtling you forward. It is the way of fire. It is the fringe on your summer-worn cutoffs; your bare thighs a glowing smolder. What is it that calls you: the rage and grit of the waves; an unseen shore; the cool, dark depths out beyond the breakers? Or is there some other reason I cannot follow: your path through the stalks as seamless as fire, as quiet as water as you cross over the river into the welcoming arms of night?

Love in Another Season

No matter when I awake, I am a day behind—each small moment already pregnant with our separate lives. On Mt. Ruapehu the air is strong and frighteningly pure but at my depth, there is nothing to breathe but pollen and water. Please keep me abreast of the gypsies and dwarves—all things magic. When I can drift to the ledge of sleep, I can almost taste the great rounds of Mahoe and Matatoki you served us for dinner before I surrendered to a different story: we shed all of our tears—faded away; all of that love and nothing to say. The nights were filled with smoke and music, but the notes we knew wouldn't ferry desire through workday crowds. I don't know why my courage ended on the icy edge of your tallest mountain or how it slipped to the valley below: please forgive me if I wander: the moon is full here, and the night is warm: my heart's expanding beyond the window and only the clock refuses to change. Though I've created this lonely dream, don't despise my awkward silence: I need you so beautiful, glistening from the shower, and walking toward me.

Shadow of Sirius

Not you unloading groceries from the trunk of your car. Not you drinking wine on your porch as the whole of your day hums on the back of your tongue like the song of the river— a lover's kiss. Not you, but what keeps you; your silhouette against the moon.

When the mechanic popped the hood of my car, I'd hoped he'd replace the linkage, reset the timing, erase the blacktop of my past—turn something old to something different.

Virginia is for Lovers, the bumper sticker offers—a state of persistent desire unfulfilled: the mountains pining for the coast; the coast falling for the sea; but then what?

Tonight, I'm again unseen. The cold forgets me. The wind grumbles, indifferent. The moon remains focused on the river. In its current I can see your face—your eyes an array of flowers, each flower in bloom, each bloom a separate sweetness; a sweetness I can share only with the moon.

What Love Comes To

An arrow can never reach its target because the distance it must travel can be divided into an infinite number of sub-distances. ZENO OF ELEA

This part of morning, light wavers like the antiqued glass that surrounds our day, subtly distorts how we see our lives, forgets our need for bold-faced clarity—the maps that guide us past fallen signposts, under fading stars. It's not that we forget our way, only the landmarks: our bare feet on fresh-cut fescue; the taste of salt on a sunburnt cheek; how we all have failed. This time of morning, things sound different: the hum of the lights, a gentle snore; the tick of the heater, your hands on the keyboard at your empty desk; each thump of my heart, another apple fallen to the ground ripe and uneaten. Soon we'll say *the forsythia's budding,* turn our faces to the warming sun, sniff the air—as if that would tell us where we should go. One small thing I still love about you is how little of you that I actually know: I know you from your sisters, but just beyond that, when your self-conscious stare becomes downward glance, I can only say beautiful, and know what it means for you to round the corner of morning, deeply breathe before you sigh, as if to say *this is what we have—the infinite distance between my arrow and your heart.*

American Woman

Sure they can measure the speed of sound, light, just as sure as they'll know the split of Alinghi each time she rounds another orange buoy. And yes, the captain will tell us he could sense her desire for victory as they sped down the stretch, but what is the measure of that? I, lonely here among the linen and deck shoes, would like to know; just how fast does desire travel? Are my innermost secrets racing across space & time to finally determine if it will be you who ascends these steps to wait in line for martinis, place your wager? If you were to appear, I think I'd refuse to trim the main sail, jettison my desire for polite conversation, tack toward backstreet brawl. Without you, I'm unanchored, drifting down alleys, beneath the docks, where I'm followed by merchant marines, the perfume of smelt and brine—almost beautiful if there were moonlight. I'm weak and I've created a world so fragile that the boy with the biggest heart has fallen through the hull of my boat to the cold, salty sea where, if he could, he would take it all into his mouth leaving me soft sand to walk on, somewhere firm to set my feet, which is crazy, I know, but so is desire and what we do with it. And today, alone, I desire nothing more than warm seas and gentle winds to fill my sails, carry me towards the horizon that is you.

Tree of Smoke

I want to believe there was smoke, a spark—but there wasn't.
You were simply consumed—another gift at a Chinese funeral.
By the time I arrived, the house was empty—even the lilies
refused to bloom. But up in the sky, the past shined ahead,
humming a song we forgot to learn.

I've trained my ear to hear the horizon note of your eyes—iridescent like dragonfly wings; how we imagine the hummingbird. Is that all there is for us to count on, the pull of desire—our calloused hands never quite soft or strong enough?

In the dark of the yard, the lilies knot, change direction; the moon rises despite grief's weight. I know you better than anyone else: two old chairs alone in the kitchen—dust settling around us.

Summer Sutra

Under threat of summer showers and vows I fear will be broken, sitting here means to be more alone than alone—like the velvet black mole who softens the dark soil of the garden until a failing faith in his own heart noses him upward to the blinding sun. In your absence, I can only wait: wait for the lightning to turn the air a bit sweeter, the rain to tease the roof from its ticking to a softer song—a litany that cries for your return. And I too have called out to the evening, been answered by the martins' swoop & gorge—the seamless resurrection of the mosquitoes' swarm; but what am I to learn from all of this? Right now, you could be kneeling on the far side of this world practicing calligraphic sutras for love, your host holding his affection—a seamless moment from the day you first met. Do you remember the very first thing that you ever wrote just for me—your name in looping blue ink? I kept that note in my pocket until the paper turned soft as linen—the words faded and returned to their space in your heart. This summer, the swallows have returned once again to their nest in our barn—I watch them stalk flies for the fledglings as the lilies summer and fold.

Unlocking the Air

More often now, it seems, we're on the edge of winter—even in memory: Richmond & Manassas—every place one can stand just long enough that even its failures have a place in your heart; like that gentle slide to the empty brightened landscapes of winter: the bumblebee abandoned hedges, the vacant eaves, and, in the trees, the silent nests. Across the river, an Eastern hemlock stands alone, weighted in wisdom and I remember how the oaks of the Edisto seemed like that, though I didn't care much then: eighteen, rushing headlong toward better things; even now, I can't resist—speeding past what's meant to be our greatest desire: the float of perfume as we open our eyes, the chorus of the tide & the sides of a boat steadily churning the current's pull—all of the moments that survived our prowl, call out to us now.

Breaking the Glass

Early October: the tenuous farewell of late afternoon and Sunday brunch on the screened-in porch; everywhere bruised & battered beech and maple—elms and willows already naked. Six months of green fading from our home and soon the faint smell of smoke, and soon frost on windows; soon, too, the musty odor of long-locked interiors—reason enough to deflate and pack my swollen heart. In the yard you tilt mother's pitcher above your head—cascading light through which our lives seem to glow & sing. But as I watch, the yellow moon of old betrayals drifts overhead and fog descends, shrouding our yard & fall & you, and I cannot keep my eyes from rejecting this vision of love. At once you recede to a tiny point: an old TV whose plug is pulled. Only fear is left as witness—that sour taste of misguided indulgence; a stellar black hole draining my world. And so in the end, it comes to this: this is the center of my heart: empty and dark with the cold of space forever expanding between me and you.

Sometimes Winter Comes When
You Least Expect It

Like a winter day that arrives in June when there's nothing to do but drink black coffee, watch the rain, so too will the thin white inch of memory round your neighbor's corner, disappear down the block. Like touching my finger to your lips, so too will the day-long mist sharpen something for us, perhaps our image of how life could be on a different street. St. Francis stands by the birdbath, his arms opened to us. If not for the rain, I'd call it a miracle. The wind gusts, obscuring your face, any thoughts as to why we remain so devoted to the return of winter—its forced isolation. That thin white inch—is it a wound that will never heal, a promise continually broken? My finger breaks the mirrored water, soothes your lips—a healing you desire, but for reasons that are all my own.

Explorers

It is early and rain drips into the blue birdbath; the sun is just beginning to rise and I cannot forget what has become of our once tied futures. You were crying again late last night, and I think I can see the salt from your tears mapping the leaves of our Japanese maple. If I were to follow the roughened path, might I find the secret that churns your lasting sadness?

I have been watching a mosquito harvest blood from my wrist for minutes—for hours. This is no exaggeration. The blood pulses through its nose like a river—like time.

Alone at night, I often dream that you float from our footed tub into the garden without ever stopping; and when the moon slips through the trees, you turn to water.

It is early and you are sleeping at the bottom of the world while I traverse our garden thumbing what little remains of the ripened grapes. Are those your tears that explore my arms when I dare to squeeze just past hard? All night long, a late fall rain drizzled our garden. The swollen fruit hasn't been picked in weeks. Nothing has grown in weeks.

Only fools think they can carry a handful of water around the world. Will you know it's me when I find you there? Will you know it's me when I show you the leaf from our Japanese maple?

Train Dreams

Today, winter has returned, the crocus has collapsed, the nearripe rosebuds frozen like the sunken sky. And we're outside with our two dogs, who circle your feet as you stand by the car—rain pimpling your naked legs, sliding inside your kneehigh boots. Rain fills my slippers too, as I follow your eyes, to the pearled buttons of your wrinkled shirt. The train's distant whistle cries beyond the edge of town but I've been carried so far from this dreary moment that its lament, and your words, fall to the ground like last summer's lilies. I've gone to a place that's just as cold as the afternoon that you first disappeared from my heart; the sharp winter sun cutting the branches of the leafless trees, igniting the buildings that lined the sidewalk. You were framed by the burning glass—shining the way camellias shine, glazed in ice—walking away, as you are now. Don't you realize that this leaving does not fade when you round the corner? That it keeps returning, like this winter that seems to have turned to one long season?

New River Breakdown

Just past June and our old dog is swimming the slow summer waters of this ancient river; both of them gliding with a natural ease that defies their age, the intent and purpose of their separate journeys. Closing my eyes, I can't help but imagine you on your trip, thumb gently stroking your oneway passage across Cook Straight. In pea coat and cap, on the back of the boat you seem to be looking for where you have been as a pod of small dolphins jumps & dives in the wake of your southbound ferry. It's hard to imagine that kind of freedom: happy both in & out of the water. But even those dolphins, their gray rounded fins like worn river rocks, are harder and harder to find. Up on the ridge in the hazy distance, a wild goat surveys her bend in the river. If given just one more chance, do you think she would jump in the farmer's old pickup—enjoy the fenced safety of stables and hay? After the ferry has docked in Picton, the strong brave arms of someone else will start to warm your restless heart. So, before you've forgotten what you've left behind, I want you to know how far I have come: I still like to feel rooted—find comfort beneath the outspread branches of hundred-foot trees. But there's also the river, moving on to Virginia; and each time our dog circles back past me, I can see in her eyes that she wants me to follow, see just how far it can possibly take us.

Music Like Dirt

For as long as I can remember, perhaps before, I have been infatuated with these pecan trees. Mistaken their knots and wounds for eyes, ears, which, in this country, is becoming easy. Their roots will never abandon us. I'm enamored of the centipede, how its long fingers weave together like a favored grandparent's: ready to cushion our first falls, shield us from the emptiness of our futures. And I admire the squeaky black mole, passionately burrowing beneath the grass, devouring termites & maggots and other malignancies never brought to light. Is there life without the swoop and dive of the gull, its feathers glowing brilliant and white in the noonday sun? Without the reliable waves frothing clean on the shore? Let me stay here forever. Let the black sand and dogwood blooms sustain me. Let the night rest lightly upon my face, the cool scent of dew parting my parched lips. I understand why the robin does not leave for winter, its head dutifully cocked to the ground—listening. I am in love with the family cemetery. The green grass weaving an afghan of warmth for those grown thin with age. The live oak holds sentry—its roots reaching out, binding us tightly together. And I am not afraid when new monuments sprout from the soil. No matter the names, I am happy, overjoyed even. I can claim the calm and peace of the handcrafted bass or fiddle—the knowledge of my own distinct sound and range—my undisputed moment in this song.

✳ ✳

It don't matter what I do
If I win or if I lose
Sweetheart I'm nothing without you
STEVE EARLE

Man on the Moon

Like the ending flourish of that piece by Shostakovich that she loves but can never recall, first one, seven, then the rest of her guests descend the steps where she sits, her head all vibration, the spin of the party still moving through it. The darkened windows across the street pull her in as she warms to the light of the arching moon, leans forward, tries to hide in the fog of her winter breath—and yes, she is in love with him, and no, he does not know it—and he stares through his window at the moon's slow ascent, its deep bruises and scars, and the stars pop on, flicker, tease the dark—the streets slowly draining until the hum of the night bus, empty on its route, seems normal, as natural as breathing—and for a moment they are together in this clarity of desire. But this is not that, this is loneliness: the moon taking root in the sky, silence in silence, the stars, and beyond them: ice and darkness—the place where the slow fear of love emanates.

The Echo Maker

Because he can still see the embodiment of his desire, and still knows your love through a memory that is both vibrant as sweat-wetted skin and yet, utterly false—like how the warmth of your whisper across the room seemed erotic as your tongue on the lobe of his ear, if only in that part of his mind filling slowly with lint, pennies, and seeds—he hates how he can't resist your gaze as you were, before, when a moment is nothing like need made flesh through movement or intention as when, near the end of a drought, the lilies still struggle to hold themselves open for whatever the morning will offer of its dew.

Maps & Atlases

And for her too, there was this steady pulse to look beyond the
world she knew: the dusty shelves, the books—walls peppered
with maps of symbols, numbers, borders beyond the breadth
of her imagination; and this desire: always in evenings, in
exhaustion, in such traffic that highways warp & bend, power
grids slip off the horizon to reveal, not the world she dreamed,
but magnified & warped—as through a fishbowl, a funhouse
mirror; and being so close, she feels its sharp taste back up in her
throat and its song from her stomach croons, "take me back…"
until she's amazed at the shades of brown in the eyes of the
man on the bike, the unplumbed depths in the black of his hair,
the softness in the calloused hand reaching toward her—and
she would have stepped out, gone with him—wherever that
was—but that his reaching was the point.

Daydream Believer

She has gone to the windfarmer again. They are riding the bareback palomino toward the peak of his acreage. Beauty caresses her face, runs through her hair as he explains the mechanics of electricity, his dreams of the sheep he will one day add to his growing operation. The sun always rests to the right of his fields; the wind gathers just enough that you sense its presence—a guardian angel, a woman's intuition. It's not that he's smarter than you; it's the loftiness of his ideals. It is that he's smarter than you. You have no interest in wind or wool: don't know a sheer from an updraft, a wether from a dam. By now the palomino is grazing far down the slope and they are making love on the shady side of the largest outcropping. Her clothes form a tail to the coarse wool blanket conveniently forgotten. It's not that she doesn't love you—that's what bursts your inflated heart. It's that today, like the breeze in the city, you're not even a passing thought.

Like Rain on a Sunny Day

As if it were then, through the steam of the rain, at the 7-Eleven, in the mid-afternoon, of late July, early August—time when water leaps from itself—you see her unexpectedly, putting gas in her station wagon, air in a tire, while her daughter watches on; and for a moment, you catch her smiling unguarded, and you try to recall the color of her eyes, but the afternoon rain and summer sun collide so that all you have now is the nape of her neck, the curve of the shoulders that you remember from before—maybe her ears, the small of the back—but then the cashier wants to know if you've found what you need, if you want something else—but this is not about desire, this is not regret—no, this is not that at all.

Tin

It's a long time to wait for a snapshot she had no reason to send. Perhaps her old camera finally refused to answer its calling. Perhaps she moved from apartment to apartment, house to house, hoping to find just the right background. Perhaps each time she set up the tripod, she became so enraptured by the natural beauty off in the far distance that she just couldn't bear to place herself in it. Perhaps, on the morning she took this, she woke up dreaming of all of the lives that she left behind. The picture she sent is black & white: and from the way that she looks toward the edge of the landscape, you can imagine how yellow the ripened lemons; and off on the peak of that distant mountain, the snow is melting—tears that run until they join the river that cuts the town in the valley below. Maybe just then she thought to remember the first night your puppy slept away from its litter; how her tiny whimpers grew persistent and loud until she burst to a howl. This was a moment when nothing else mattered—the depths of loneliness easily answered with the simplest of acts: holding head to chest. Maybe when she awoke, the grass was so green with the morning dew that the lemons were singing in the peak of their tartness—but not for her; and so she took it, freezing forever, her unending song, in hopes of finding your distant heart.

Midnight Salvage

But now, everything is quiet: the shouts that once bounced from the dew-fogged glass of your neighbors' windows; the tears that—like storms on the coast—needed no front to howl and tumble: the air here calm and deep like the moment just after you're kissed or the breath of a woman asleep in her bed: what some would name desire, but is more; place in which—without intention—you've been welcomed, feel a resonance: like receiving a call in a foreign country and, when you answer, your reply tumbles out with perfect inflection; an answer that—without practice—you knew without thinking. This is the end of your pilgrimage; this is clarity: what you never knew you needed but reached for all along.

Watching the Spring Festival

And with that, it's all gone: food, music, time; the beach-house, imagined; your voice, the fog after sunrise; I've turned to the déjà vu of fresh-cut grass—not in spring, but October. No dogs, butterflies, finches at the feeder; the ivy's overtaken St. Francis, the birdbath's broken: it's the curse of Adam, the gift of Eve: work, love—the bone-weary weight of guilt: wrapping ourselves in grandmother's quilt, our song becomes the barbed wire that fences our borders: love is bartered for work: knotted ties, pressed shirts—the way we speak and say nothing. I remember the reed-soft ballad of the nylon-stringed guitar; your hair, face, aglow with the cold: you rounded the corner of winter like an album grooved to last for just one season. That music we played, can you see how it turned? Now tongueless— eyes wide as a pelican's mouth—I can take it all in: beauty bought with handshakes and false flatteries, shipped on buses from exotic places where the gloss is more important than the lips, highlights what's recalled of the hair—the music all digitized. What happened to the silence of fresh-powdered snow—each flake as pure as daybreak, as new as our days together? What turned true; was it really wrong?

Listen

It takes patience for something good to turn clear and true: and
I don't wish for my love returned, not anymore—dreaming each
night it was all mistake. The mind moves toward wakefulness,
tunes to the record left on all night, the scrape of the street
sweeps through the screened door; otherwise, it's unseasonably
quiet—no birds, the pollen a dampening yellow. Today I've
learned the measure of a season's distance, discovered the heart
I knew I had; a truth beguiled. The birds return with their
summer mantra: sand & salt, salt & sun—my heart's healed
over. Would you have been, in other times, the music that seems
to haunt these lines? This is what I've learned of possibility:
you left me with what you tried to save me from; and I am
equal to that rejection: the mockingbird whose mimicked song
is still an arrow that seeks the heart.

* * *

I've got my problems
Sometimes love don't solve them
BONNIE "PRINCE" BILLY

The Common Man

High summer: the leaves in the treetops flash white in warning and you, who are not yet my wife, turn your face to the darkening sky and ask, *Can you smell it?* Years later, I will head our basil before driving to see you; and amid the jokes of JELL-O and bedpans you'll ask me again, *Can you smell it?* But we are not so old, not just yet; and you are just a girl from up the street. It is mid-July and you're on your toes stretching your body toward the gathering ozone like it's freshly whipped cream or magnolia blossoms. It will be many years before I remember this day: how when the rain came, you grabbed my hands spinning us both round & round; how when the lightning struck the tree by the house and the hair on my neck stood on end; how I knew at that moment for the very first time that fear and love were one and the same.

The Bright Forever

You will be leaving soon, drifting to where you cannot find me—our days a flock of blackbirds gone south for the winter. I miss already your words at play: laughter that breaks the skin of the river again & again. Behind the house, smoke drifts from the neighbor's chimney, the birdbath's empty—I have no words for this: I am lost in the crunch and click of the frost—its voice an accusation: I do not want you to forget my name but when you do, promise to remember what we had, to linger in every goodbye like the last wren at the feeder, like the salt on your skin after making love. Our time together was marked by more laughter than tears—these notes, they'll continue sailing; there is nothing else like them.

Delight & Shadows

Just past the alarm, I lie half-awake wishing for sunlight to shimmy and dance behind the dull frost on my bedroom window. Here, winter is when the sky hesitates at gray for hours, sunrise a deep wound that slowly leaches up and outward. If I can drift close enough to sleep, I can see our last night unfold around us, miss nothing of your hands strong on my stomach, your breath in my ear, as we watch distant mountains spark and then burn in that fiery instant peaks are transformed by the clarity of morning. But here, the haze slows us all in its yellowed ether: robins and wrens stay tucked in their nests, the belch of the bus hangs thick as the traffic. The peaks of the Alps, your voice in the air, are no longer glowing—flush with the warmth of what used to be our new life together.

In Other Rooms, Other Wonders

The thing is, her beauty comes from what she's left behind, how it shines through the selfless body of the woman she always wanted to be, sipping mussels from their salty shells as if she were the ocean itself. I throw a handful of whitened bones into the dirt only to find the same answer; but there, where music is the smell of a wave as it hurls itself against the shore, the future doesn't matter. There is only the black sand. There is only the whale's eye, reflecting in its darkness the sunken boat of the fisherman; and we are stowed safely aboard—the mussels, somehow alive in their shells, our passage home, like guardian angels, no more for now than warm dogs asleep on the bed.

Sand & Gravel

Even when your breath tasted of whiskey—your body pressing mine to the frozen earth—you could make me quiver. Everything was upside down over there: the deep fragrant clouds of our lovely breathing heavy as June—the beginning of winter; I heard snow falling and yes, guitars—our bare skin, stars on black sand—pomegranate stained our hungry fingers, mouths with secrets. And now I know why I wanted lilac, honeysuckle scenting the steam as we tried to wash ourselves clean of each other: if I could go back to then, it would still be with you, with me, dreaming your cold bed warm.

The Surrendered

The rain sheets the beach and we are content; Main Street vanished, our home forgotten. The teenaged waitress over at Marvin's, she too is happy. I can tell by the way her eyes outshine her silver studs, the lilt in her step when she brings our fish and mug after mug of beer. Back in our room, we shrug off our shirts and catalog chinos, lie naked on the cotton spread. For fifty cents, the bed vibrates and we are alone once again: you on a train to Coromandel; I'm up on a ladder patching the roof of our first house, the shingles shivering in the March wind. At midnight, I awake to silence: who did I think I'd be by now? And what do I do with who I am? See you tomorrow, the girl had said, her voice rising just enough. Outside the rain has finally stopped. You part the glassy surface of the lowest tide I've ever seen. The moon silvers your skin.

Practical Gods

The evening sun reflects off our blue birdbath, the memory of afternoon rain, as the day's end is marked on an empty wall; the leaky gutter still crying, inconsolable—like a mother who has just found, or lost, her only child (a fact I only mention because, from our bed, it always seems to be raining). There is no point to this: my wife does not want a child; the weather does not reflect unknown desire. If she were home, I would undress her in the cooling light, the tears from the willows glistening on her skin. But she is in a different season, and I am here alone. What would happen next, I will not say. You should know that the blue birdbath has the slightest of cracks and is always glazed with rain—make what you want of it. There is only one robin that visits our yard—her breast its own sunset. At dusk she hops from puddle to puddle—listening.

Silence

It is not the sand or receding tide, heavy with salt, that I am thinking of, my hands rubbing my eyes as if they were some genie's lamp, my wishes with me all along. No, I am thinking of rain at the end of winter—what a comfort it is to find hope in the hopeless like repetition, like ice. I am thinking of the cardinal who tries to fly through that just-cleaned window, how good it must feel to finally forget, resting your head on the cool cement. I am thinking of Cassandra, whose story's so tragic, it could only have come from a guilty heart. I am thinking of silence, the silence I hear when your name is a question, your absence somehow making this room quieter than ever before.

Where I'm Calling From

Is life lived better there, where nightly you gather together around tables like the cast of a play—the bright colors of your conversation glowing like the feathers of a tropical bird or the neon lights of Las Vegas. The walk back to your meager rooms cuts through alleyways and across a river—the oils of the night burning off with the sunrise. Here, as in that part of the world, the morning light has a way of coaxing the spirit free of itself: squirrels seem to float more than fall through the tender spring shoots of the elms to the rooftop, the too-red cardinal sings through the tangled enterprise of confederate jasmine on the arbor—works to ease the burden of the encroaching summer, all our unreasonable fears.

How Long?

This one, I don't have: you, back at the airport, the stamps on your passport so varied, so rich, the clerk in customs seems to be glowing. I'd like to say here that your eyes are deep blue, like the skies in the country after a storm. But that would be lying; I only remember the deepest of grays, like in that lost picture: feet on the rail of grandmother's porch—you could be her back then, if the soles of your shoes were filled with black mud, didn't say ALL-STAR.

It hurts to think that most of our lives fall somewhere between the rush of full color and the fading memory of black & white—between fucking & love. Someone once told me every picture we take steals a small fragment of the subject's soul. Is that where we gain our darkest addictions: backpackers, musicians, the drunken reporter whose laughter and stories we'd like to obtain—that impossible paycheck received without guilt, without anger?

On the edge of the river, you can find tall grass, a lonely shepherd, and sometimes, I suppose, a warm wool blanket. But those escapes are just for you, you alone. My love is an overturned lantern, terribly empty. My love is behind the counter at the pharmacy window. Are you still searching for the best choice of words to translate my secret? Do you really believe I could keep something from you?

For some, there is an empty tomb. Still others hope to sleep beneath that holy tree. I dedicate myself to the here and now: leaves peeling from the tired elms, yard overgrown with cherry tomatoes, burnt coffee and sirens waltzing on the predawn air. Like a forgotten orchard off a lonely blacktop, my aching branches are full and heavy. Won't you come find me? Stay for the season?

Harbor

I don't know who I thought I was back then, but the afternoon sun sifted through the Spanish moss that curled from the trees with the natural grace of girls in August. It could be like that: the breeze fanning the gnats from the palms, the palms lulling the stars to sleep. I wanted to be your last dream before waking. I wanted the blanket of night to be as soft and clean as an infant; our love to be as bright and clear as the moon when it bursts through the floor of dusk's horizon. I'm still not sure if I was living the life I wanted to believe or the life I believed I wanted but even the waves at highest tide seemed to slow and kiss the shore. Remember that dive that collapsed to the water? Someone had carved LOVE IS GRAVITY into our table. Is that the force that grounds us? Or keeps us from ascending? The love we have is the song of the fiddler crab as it backs its way into its hole. I remember how bright the beach could be late at night—each star pointing to unseen places for love to hide. Remember the dolphins in early morning—the steady rhythm as they surfaced & dove, surfaced & dove, surfaced & dove— their work a constant reminder of death and resurrection? I doubt I thought of it like that then—how natural it is for love to die and return again. I just wanted our hearts to continue expanding. It was the gulls who finally showed me that, at the edge of our world, there is another. Love never really dies; it becomes the fog that blankets the sunrise; the silence between our conversations. The highway off that little island split in two unjoined directions—as if to give us a final choice: it's the love we have. It's the raft I choose when the rising tide is you.

Complicated Mathematics

Make it seven years ago. Meet me in the middle of the street. I know I'll be wobbly—a bit unsure, like blackbirds in the vineyard just after harvest. But you, you will get it right: the cheekbones, breasts; your voice glowing like maples in fall, like now. It's just the disorder—the earliness of it all. It worries me. The greenness, the focus it takes to tread water; everything reduced to the sound of the ocean trapped in a shell, which is just to say: when your voice breaks free, becomes that one clear note, I will be afraid. But then you'll appear as you should— like tulips in spring, and we'll agree that the sky looks bluer in the morning, unpolluted, as sunset speaks beauty to the night.

Time & Material

The final turn between earth and sky, the length of your body rises up from mine—your bare skin railing against the lonely ending of our fallen lives. And because I can no longer touch your breasts, I picture them instead: soft, pale, nipples stiff with wind. Tell me, there must be a reason this world still needs all we have—orchards rotting away to snow filled winters; the white hills mottled with leaves and tracks. Clouds smudge the pastures as if grief were leaking from the peaks of mountains, over their barren edges, to puddle below. I did not say this then, but I want to now: how clearly I knew our days together could not outlast the tides or seasons. And yet no knowledge or premonition can split the fabric of grief & time. Isn't that the impossible truth of what it means to fall in love? How in all the pictures we cease to change, even as our hearts depart this world, leaving only memory, calling, *Closer, come closer?*

Different Hours

We are fathoms deep into winter here. The sound of the sleet on our porch pushes pools of water toward the basement door. Nothing's dry to the touch. Since I did not follow you, the road from here will remain hidden. And since I did not follow you, I find I'm becoming more and more like you—cloud whose rain never stops falling, never touches the ground. Swimming at night is lonely and sad—old age: with no achievements or dreams, we float just above & below the surface. The ice moans in the black branches of the dormant elms. This is the season of forgotten ghosts. Like martyred prophets, the bearded trees rebuke the moonlight. It's neither the end nor beginning of all we hope for. Our lives will continue forward until we form a vertical circle: immortality has nothing to do with avoiding death. It is better I did not follow. How else would we meet again?

Evidence of Things Unseen

In the dream, there's a forgotten pasture I can't stop finding, just as, when I'm there, I can't stop feeling at ease, at home— and isn't that, before, what it was? Familiar clearing at the edge of the wilderness, who's centered oak created shade and, much later, lightning? As for family—Yes—and all of them—and with little variation each struggling to brush the fallen hair from her face or hoping, if only briefly, someone would touch his hand. I live—like I live; they do what they can for me. It's as if we're all worth loving, and worth forgiving, both. In the dream, there's a forgotten pasture I can't stop finding—and often, family, waiting there with a gesture of tenderness: fingers on my cheek, resting lightly, making me want, almost, to pull someone (myself?) back. I can feel all the washed out stones, start to whisper deep inside me, their faded verse singing.

Waiting

And yet, I rest uneasily here, between these four flagged posts, where the lilies resurrect each spring, fence slowly sagging toward the post oak—sentinel to my sleeping; and often at night, housecats moan and embrace their feral lovers; and often in morning, I'll pad the rows of the heirloom garden—ears gently perked to the cardinal's whistle, the cucumber's creeping. In preparation, I've planted shade trees at every corner, flowers along the fence; and I've swept the porch of pollen and seeds, chilled white wine; and still . . . I can't describe this: a glitch in the magnetic field, the moment before you sneeze, the instant the match hits charcoal—that sort of blue? Someone's crying— a trail of salt etches the laughlines of my face; someone swings a rake from the shadows but I'm just too tired to tense for the blow; and all the while, the latch on the gate slowly rusts open. Tomorrow, I'll lie in bed and watch the rain drip from the leaves of the glowing elms; I'll spend what's left of summer's daylight measuring the distance from memory to happiness; and when I find the answer, I'll dress unseasonably in knit & corduroy, so you'll know that it's me.

Servant of the Map

Because there is nothing we can do but cry for the brightest stars, smooth the crumpled map. Because there is nowhere left to go that will make the rain feel colder, make me fear the knot behind my eye until it hurts; because the dogs have removed the woodpile, log by rotting log, lost it to the current of the river. Because they have pulled your dirty socks from the wicker hamper, made a bed to cry themselves to sleep. Because I have come to call you forsythia, I have tattooed the blossoms of early spring across my naked heart. I count the blackbirds in the sleeping elm—wish them safe passage through a year that is sure to be stillborn. There is smoke in the air as I gulp the first breaths of morning. This is our elegy of hair, of fingernails, of dust. The wind has found home in the cup of my hand. The river erases a path through the muddied landscape. Your voice echoes through the fog, covers my body like a corduroy coat. What else is left to do? I'll start walking.

Terry L. Kennedy is the author of the limited edition chapbook *Until the Clouds Shatter the Light That Plates Our Lives*, selected by Thomas Lux for Jeanne Duval Editions of Atlanta, GA. His work appears in numerous literary journals and magazines including *Cave Wall, from the Fishouse, Southern Review,* and *Waccamaw,* and has been honored with a Randall Jarrell Fellowship as well as fellowships to the Virginia Center for the Creative Arts. He currently serves as the Associate Director of the Graduate Program in Creative Writing at the University of North Carolina at Greensboro and is Editor of the online journal *storySouth.*

Text and titles printed in Adobe Caslon. Cover and text designed by Andrew Saulters.

The author signed 26 hardbound copies, lettered A through z. An additional 100 hardbound copies and 375 bound in paper were produced by Unicorn Press in the first printing.